SEP 1 9 1998

NOV – 5 1998

NOV 5 98

8

D1405101

DEC – 8 1999

FEB 1 0 2000

APR 4 – 2000

SEP 1 8 2000

NOV 0 6 2000

OCT 1 6 2001

NOV 2 4 2002

SEP 1 5 2003

JAN 2 9 2004

OCT 1 7 2004

FEB 2 1 2005

J912S

B&T

DISCOVERING GEOGRAPHY

MAPS

DAVID L. STIENECKER

■

ART BY RICHARD MACCABE

BENCHMARK BOOKS

MARSHALL CAVENDISH
NEW YORK

Benchmark Books
Marshall Cavendish Corporation
99 White Plains Road
Tarrytown, New York 10591

©Marshall Cavendish Corporation, 1998

Series created by Blackbirch Graphics, Inc.

Printed and bound in the United States.

Photo Credits
Page 4: Library of Congress; page 5: Photodisc; page 28: ©NASA/Peter Arnold, Inc.

Library of Congress Cataloging-in-Publication Data

Stienecker, David.
    Maps / by David L. Stienecker.
        p.   cm. — (Discovering geography)
    Includes index.
    Summary: Points out the various kinds of information which different maps offer and suggests activities for further study.
    ISBN 0-7614-0538-0 (lib. bdg.)
    1. Maps—Juvenile literature. [1. Maps.] I. Title.
II. Series: Discovering geography (New York, N.Y.)
GA130.S82   1998
912—dc21   3630/377
                                                97-1455
                                                CIPxx
                                                AC

Contents

An atlas is a book of maps.

Where in the World Am I?

How do you show someone where you've been? How do you show them how to get there, or how to get back? You make a map.

As people began to explore the world, they needed maps so they could get back to the new places they discovered.

This map of the world was made about 2,000 years ago by a Greek mapmaker and astronomer called Ptolemy. Ptolemy's maps were printed in an atlas in the late 1400s. Columbus used a map like this when he accidently discovered some parts of the world that weren't on the map.

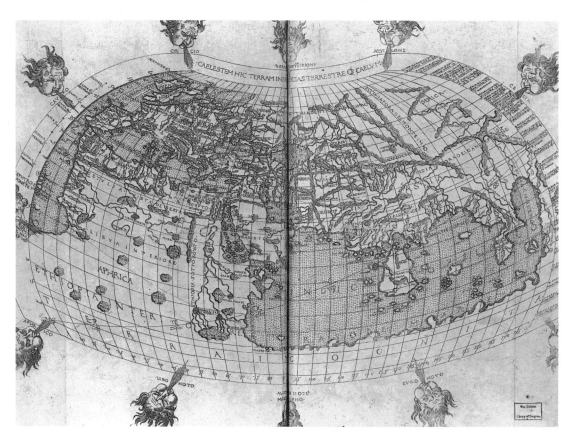

- Most of the words on Ptolemy's map are written in Latin. But see if you can find Asia, Africa, and Europe. They're spelled almost the same in Latin as in English.

After Columbus accidently landed in North America, the map of the world began to change. This map of the world was made in 1570.

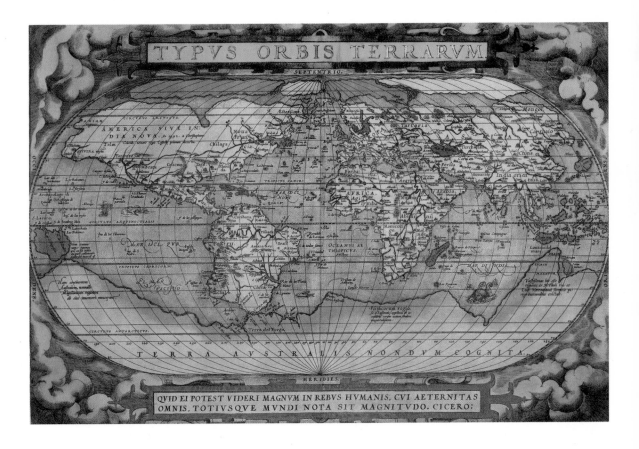

- See if you can locate North and South America.

- Compare this map of the world to Ptolemy's map. How are they similar? How are they different?

I Thought the World Was Round!

There was a time when people thought the Earth was flat. But now we know the Earth is shaped like a ball. The best way to show the Earth's land and water is by drawing a map on a ball. This type of map is called a globe.

Globes may be very accurate maps, but they are hard to fit in your pocket, and they don't lay flat on your lap. So, how do you make a flat map out of the curved surface of a globe? Try this to find out how.

1. Cut an orange in half and scoop out the inside of one of the halves so you have just the peel left.

2. Draw a picture on the peel with a marker.

3. Try making the orange lie flat without breaking it, or squashing it out of shape. What happens to your picture when you finally flatten the peel?

Your picture became distorted. It wasn't exactly the same as before. This happens when mapmakers try to make a flat map of the round Earth.

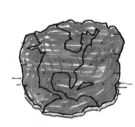

All maps have some distortion. The more of Earth's surface a map shows, the more it has been flattened out and the greater its distortion. Maps of the whole world show the most distortion. Maps of smaller areas show the least.

To make a map of the world, imagine you are peeling the surface of a globe and stretching it flat. The trick is to peel it in such a way as to have the least amount of distortion.

Here's one way to peel the surface of a globe to make a map.

First divide the globe this way.

Next imagine peeling off the surface.

Then stretch the surface flat.

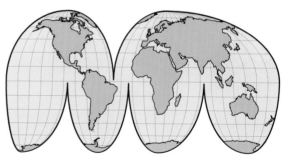

- Try doing it with an orange. You'll have better luck than the first time, but you will still have to do some stretching and pulling.

- To see the distortion in a map, compare a map of the world to a globe. Compare the shapes and sizes of the landmasses and how far apart they are.

Many Ways to Draw the Earth

Mapmakers have tried many ways of drawing the Earth. These drawings are called projections. There are many different kinds of projections. Here are a few you may have seen.

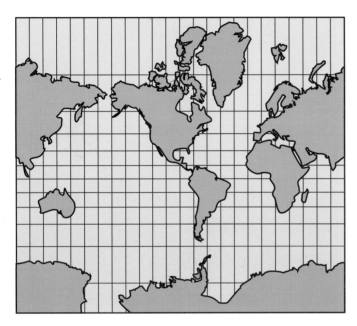

This is a Mercator projection. It shows the true shape of land areas. But the sizes are distorted. Land areas near the North and South poles (the top and bottom of the map) look much larger than they really are. Sizes of the land near the equator are more accurate.

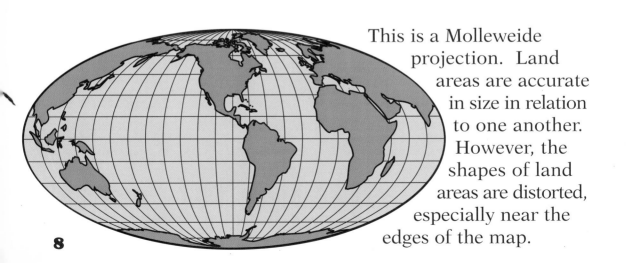

This is a Molleweide projection. Land areas are accurate in size in relation to one another. However, the shapes of land areas are distorted, especially near the edges of the map.

This is a Robinson's projection. It shows fewer distortions of all kinds, but no part of the map is perfectly accurate. As a result, it is one of the most pleasing maps to look at.

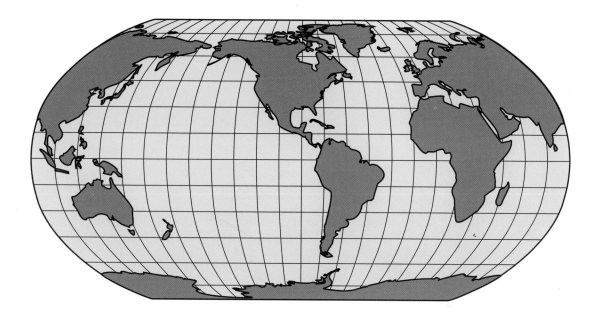

- Compare the map projections on these two pages to see how they differ. Make a chart to show the differences.

Projection	What It Shows

- Go on a map projection search. See how many different projections you can find. Keep track of them in a chart. Write down what each map shows.

Maps, Maps, Maps

When you mention maps, most people think of world maps or country maps. But there are many kinds of maps. Here are some examples of maps you may have seen, but not thought of as maps.

This is a street map. It gives the names of streets and locates important buildings and landmarks such as parks, lakes, and recreational areas. See if you can find a street map of your town.

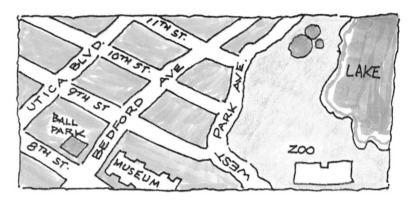

This is a park map. It shows hiking trails and biking and jogging paths. It also shows where picnic and recreational areas are located.

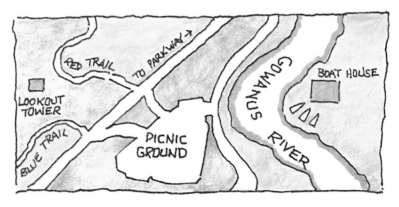

Have you ever been to a shopping mall? Shopping malls often have maps like this one. They show you how the mall is laid out and where the shops are located.

Go on a map search. Keep track of the maps you find in a chart like this. Or, take pictures of each kind of map and make a "Map Book."

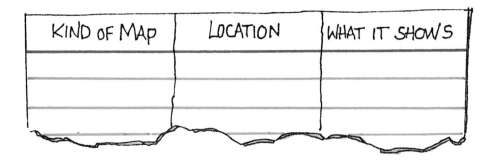

KIND OF MAP	LOCATION	WHAT IT SHOWS

Here are some ideas to get you started:

weather maps
park maps
transportation maps
neighborhood maps
state maps
museum maps

shopping mall maps
building maps
street maps
world maps
city maps
road maps

Continents and Hemispheres

The Earth's land is divided into seven continents. Locate and name the seven continents shown on this map of the world.

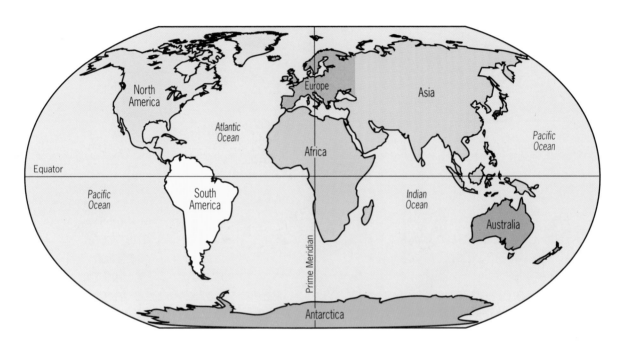

- Which continent is the largest? Which is the smallest?

- Which continents are separated by the Atlantic Ocean?

- Which continent do you live on?

Unlike the map above, when you look at a globe, you do not see it all at one time. Because it is round, you can see only half of it. The half of a globe you see is called a hemisphere, which means "half of a sphere."

The Earth can be divided into these four hemispheres.

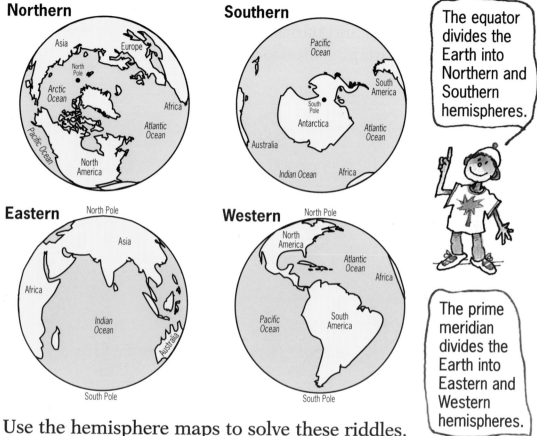

The equator divides the Earth into Northern and Southern hemispheres.

The prime meridian divides the Earth into Eastern and Western hemispheres.

Use the hemisphere maps to solve these riddles.

• All or part of me can be found in each of the four hemispheres. What continent am I?

• All or part of me is in the Northern Hemisphere and Western Hemisphere. The Atlantic Ocean is on one side of me and the Pacific Ocean is on the other side. What continent am I?

• Almost all of me is located in the Northern Hemisphere and Eastern Hemisphere. What continent am I?

Now make up some riddles of your own. Try them out on a friend.

13

The Coldest Places on Earth

The area around the North Pole is called the Arctic. It includes the Arctic Ocean, thousands of islands, and parts of Europe, Asia, and North America.

This kind of map is called a polar projection.

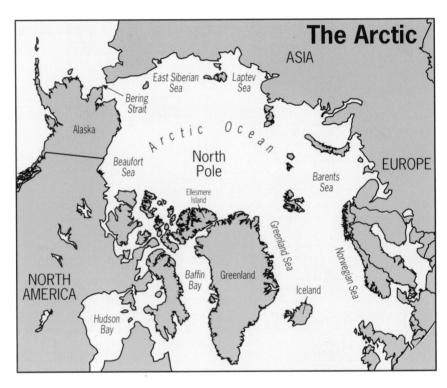

The waters around the North Pole are frozen all year. In other parts of the Arctic the snow melts during the summer months. During this time moss, lichen, berries, flowers, and vegetables grow in a few places.

- In 1909, Commander Robert E. Peary and Matthew Henson were the first people to reach the North Pole. They set out from Ellesmere Island. Locate Ellesmere Island to see the route they took.

The area around the South Pole is called the Antarctic or Antarctica. Antarctica is an ice-covered continent. It is the coldest place on Earth, even colder than the Arctic. The temperature rarely gets above 32°F (0°C). The coldest temperature was in 1983. It dropped to –128.6°F (-89°C)!

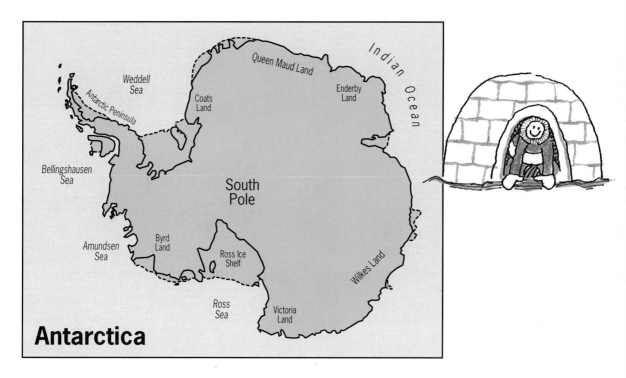

Antarctica

Antarctica contains over 90 percent of the Earth's ice and snow. In some places, the ice is 14,800 feet (4,511 meters) thick!

- In 1911, Roald Amundsen led the first expedition to reach the South Pole. He discovered it by crossing the Ross Ice Shelf. See if you can locate the Ross Ice Shelf on the map.

- Plan an exploration of the Arctic or Antarctic. List the landmarks along your route. Give your list to a friend and explore together.

The World Ocean

This is a map of the world's oceans. There are four major oceans. Can you find them on the map?

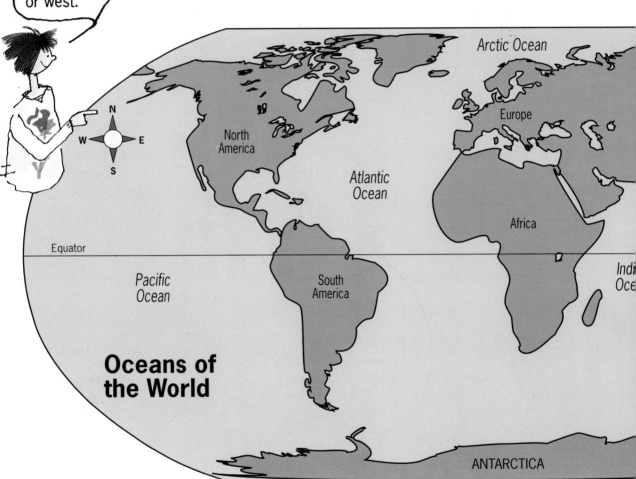

Use this compass rose to help you figure out which way is north, south, east, or west.

Oceans of the World

Arctic Ocean

Europe

North America

Atlantic Ocean

Africa

Equator

Pacific Ocean

South America

Ind[i] Oce[a]

ANTARCTICA

Let's take a trip through the oceans of the world. Use your finger to trace this route on the map.

1. Begin on the east coast of North America.

2. Head southeast across the Atlantic Ocean and sail around the southern tip of Africa.

3. Sail northeast and pass between the continents of Australia and Asia.

4. Head east across the Pacific Ocean toward the North American continent. (You'll have to move off the edge of the map and come around the other side.)

5. Sail southeast across the Pacific and around the southern tip of South America.

6. Sail up the Atlantic and back to where you began.

The world ocean is one continuous body of water that covers 70% of the Earth's surface.

Did you notice that all the oceans were connected? That's right. There is really only one world ocean. We divide it into four smaller oceans to make it easier to talk about.

• Plan some ocean trips of your own. Use direction words and the names of continents to plan a route around the world. Give your directions, along with the map, to a friend. Have your friend trace the route on the map.

Asia

Pacific Ocean

Australia

The Ocean Floor

If you were to drain the water from the oceans, you would find a landscape as varied as that on the continents. There are huge mountain ranges, long narrow valleys called trenches, plains, plateaus, steep cliffs, and canyons. The map on this page shows what part of the Pacific Ocean floor looks like.

The Pacific Ocean is bigger than the entire land surface of the Earth, covering almost a third of the Earth's surface. Its long trenches are the deepest places in the world.

- The Mariana Trench in the Pacific Ocean is the deepest known spot in all the oceans. It is 36,198 feet (11,035 meters) below the surface. Locate it on the map.

- Imagine that you are exploring the ocean floor. Plan a route of exploration using the map on the next page. Use the place names on the map to identify the route you will take.

The Hawaiian Islands were formed from volcanoes that rose from the ocean floor.

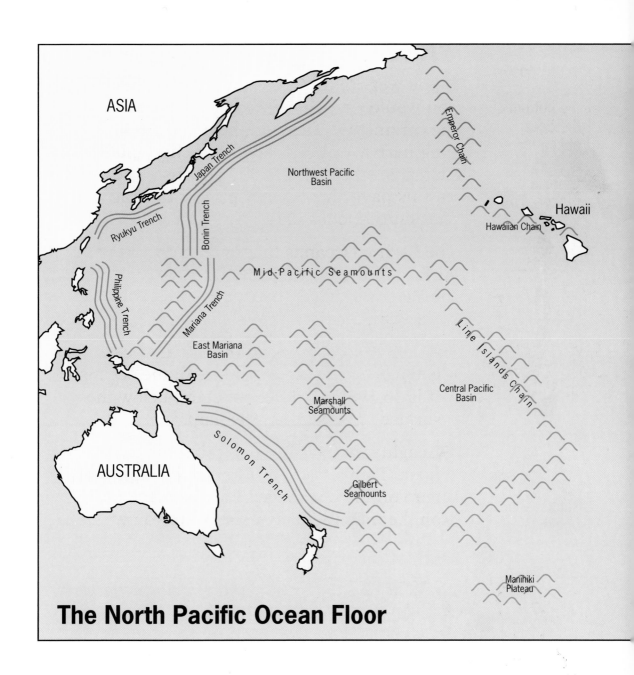

The North Pacific Ocean Floor

Treasure Hunt

If you look closely at most maps you will notice that they have lines drawn across them. They are called lines of latitude and lines of longitude.

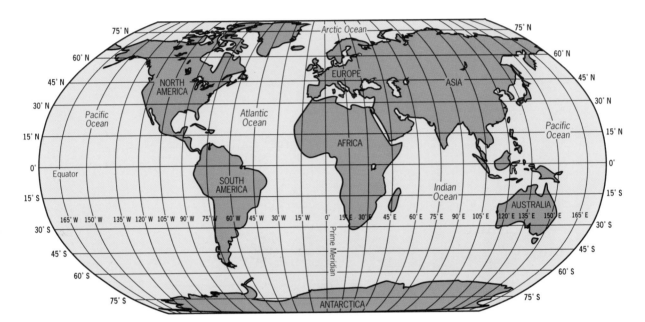

Lines of latitude and longitude are measured in degrees.

Lines of latitude run east and west. The equator is at zero degrees (0°) latitude. Other lines of latitude are used to measure how far north or south of the equator a place is.

Lines of longitude run north and south between the two poles. The prime meridian is at zero degrees (0°) longitude. Lines of longitude measure how far east or west a place is from the prime meridian.

Locate the equator and the prime meridian on this map. Then see how the lines of latitude and longitude are numbered.

20

Now let's have some fun. Use this make-believe map and the lines of latitude and longitude to discover where pirates plundered ships and buried treasure. Locate each place on the map.

• At the equator (0°) and 135° E pirates took over a ship and captured chests of gold. In what ocean did this happen?

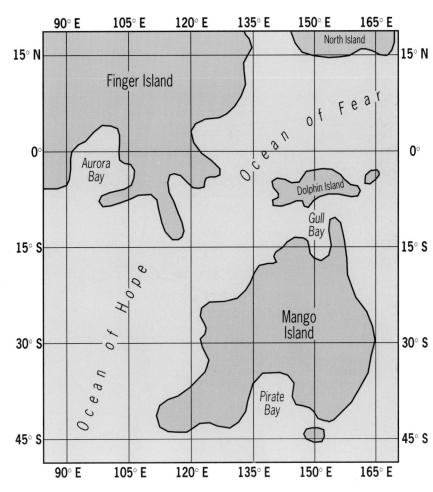

• The pirate ship sailed away and eventually buried this treasure at 30° S and 135° E. Where is the treasure buried?

• Another pirate ship with sacks of precious stones sank in a storm at 15° S and 105° E. Where did it sink?

Make up some of your own questions using this map.

Moon Map

The Earth isn't the only place that people have mapped. Can you guess what this map shows?

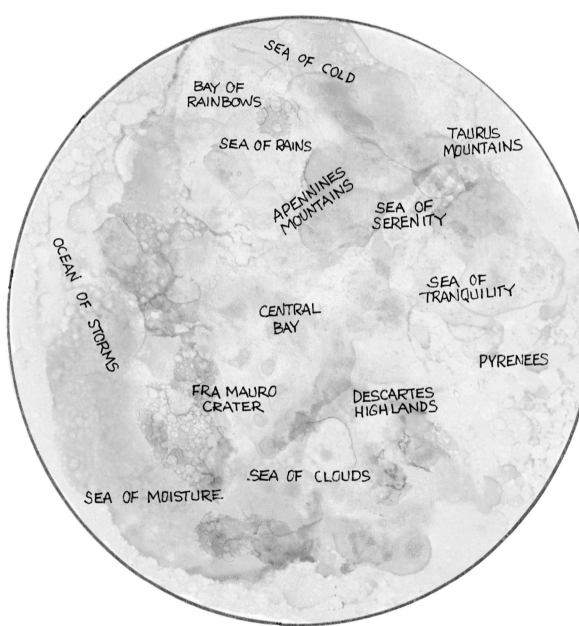

SEA OF COLD

BAY OF RAINBOWS

SEA OF RAINS

TAURUS MOUNTAINS

APENNINES MOUNTAINS

SEA OF SERENITY

OCEAN OF STORMS

SEA OF TRANQUILITY

CENTRAL BAY

PYRENEES

FRA MAURO CRATER

DESCARTES HIGHLANDS

SEA OF CLOUDS

SEA OF MOISTURE

Twelve U.S. astronauts have walked on the Moon. See if you can locate where they landed on the Moon map.

Date of Landing	Location
July 20, 1969	Sea of Tranquility
November 19, 1969	Ocean of Storms
February 5, 1971	Fra Mauro Crater
July 30, 1971	Apennines mountains
April 20, 1972	Descartes highlands
December 12, 1972	Taurus mountains

Make a Globe

You know that the best representation of the Earth is a globe. If you don't have a globe, here's a fun way to make one.

You will need:

- large, round balloon
- newspaper
- globe or world map
- mixing bowl
- water
- poster paints
- flour
- string
- markers
- hanger

What to do:

1. Blow up the balloon and tie the end so air cannot escape.

2. Hang the balloon from a coat hanger, wooden rod, or anywhere you can. Then lay some newspapers underneath the balloon. This job can get messy.

3. Tear newspaper into 1-inch strips. You don't have to be exact, but you need a lot of them.

4. Mix the flour and water to make a thick paste—about 1 cup flour to 3/4 cups water. You can add more water or flour to get it just right.

5. Dip each strip into the paste and gently pull it through your fingers to remove any excess. The strip should be completely covered with paste.

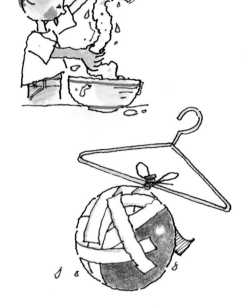

6. Lay the pasted strips on the balloon. Cover the entire balloon with several layers. If you run out of strips or paste, you can make some more.

7. Wait for the balloon to dry. It might take a day. Then paint on the oceans and continents. Copy them from a world map or globe.

8. This is what your finished globe should look like. Hang it up or set it on a table for all to admire.

Maps for Special Purposes

Sometimes maps are used to show particular things, such as rainfall, climate, population, or crops. These kinds of maps are called special purpose maps, or thematic maps. What does this map of the world show?

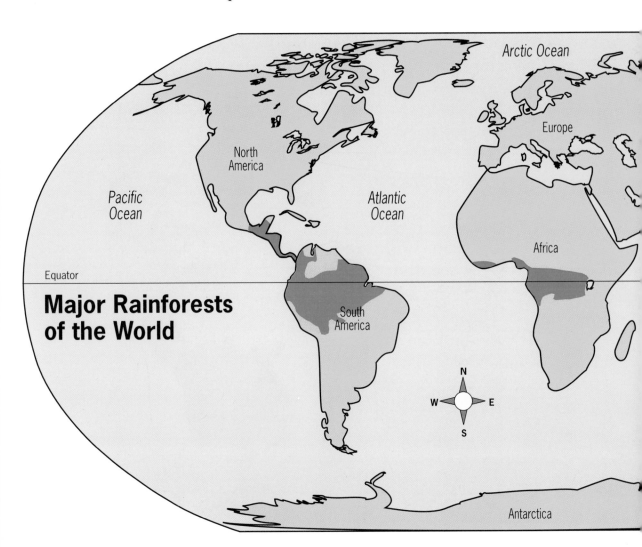

Arctic Ocean

Europe

North America

Pacific Ocean

Atlantic Ocean

Africa

Equator

Major Rainforests of the World

South America

N
W E
S

Antarctica

- The major rainforests of the world are located on four continents. Which continent has the most rainforest?

- Around what special line of latitude are most of the Earth's rainforests found?

- Make a special purpose map of your own. Your map could show the kinds of trees in your neighborhood or the kinds of stores. You could make a special purpose map to show where parks are located in the town or city where you live.

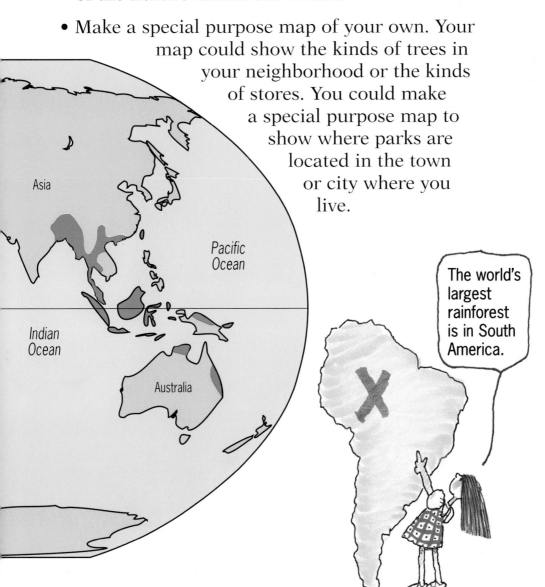

Asia

Pacific Ocean

Indian Ocean

Australia

The world's largest rainforest is in South America.

Maps from the Sky

Today, mapmakers sometimes use photographs of the Earth taken by satellites to help them make maps. This picture was taken by a NASA satellite. It shows the coastlines of Maryland, Virginia, and Delaware.

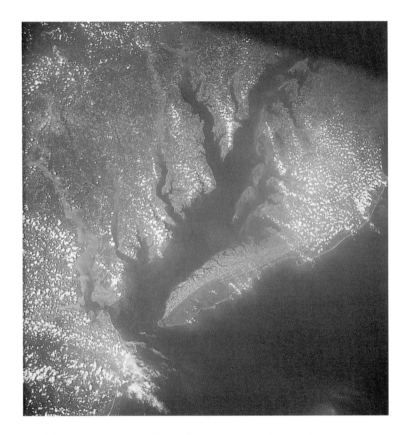

Using maps like the one above, mapmakers have been able to make more accurate maps. They have also been able to locate unmapped lakes and other natural features.

- What natural features can you identify in the picture?

- Locate a map that shows these three states. Compare it with the satellite photograph. See if you can figure out what the photograph shows.

Maps Can Be Make Believe

Maps don't always have to show real places. Sometimes maps are used to show imaginary lands that are the settings for stories. This map shows an imaginary place.

- What is the name of the make-believe place the map shows?

- What are some of the landmarks and features on the map?

- In what part of the village is Sherman Oaks?

- If the Droll Dragon wanted to swim to Kitty Island, which direction would it need to travel?

- Make up an imaginary place. Then draw a map of it. Write a story to go along with your map.

Answers

Pps. 4–5, Where in the World Am I?

The map of the world in 1570 shows North and South America, more of Africa, more of the oceans, and more accurate borders and coastlines than Ptolemy's map.

Pps. 6–7, I Thought the World Was Round!

No answers.

Pps. 8–9, Many Ways to Draw the Earth

The shapes and sizes of the continents will differ some on each map projection. Distances may also differ.

Pps. 10–11, Maps, Maps, Maps

No answers.

Pps. 12–13, Continents and Hemispheres

Asia is the largest continent. Australia is the smallest continent.

The Atlantic Ocean separates North and South America from Africa and Europe.

You live on the North American continent.

Answers to riddles: Africa, North America, Asia.

Pps. 14–15, The Coldest Places on Earth

No answers.

Pps. 16–17, The World Ocean

The four major oceans are the Atlantic Ocean, Pacific Ocean, Indian Ocean, and Arctic Ocean.

Pps. 18–19, The Ocean Floor

No answers.

Pps. 20–21, Treasure Hunt

Ocean of Fear, Mango Island, Ocean of Hope.

Pps. 22–23, Moon Map

No answers.

Pps. 24–25, Make a Globe

No answers.

Pps. 26–27, Maps for Special Purposes

The map shows the location of the major rainforests of the world.
South America.
The equator.

P. 28, Maps from the Sky

You can identify such natural features as major bodies of water, islands, rivers, and the shape of the coastline.

P. 29, Maps Can Be Make Believe

Valiant Village.

The landmarks and features are Sherman Oaks, Lake Loman, Blackwater Bay, Kitty Island, Bakingham Palace.

Sherman Oaks is in the northwest.

The dragon would travel east.

Glossary

atlas A book of maps.

compass rose A diagram on a map that shows the direction of north, south, east, and west.

continent One of seven great masses of land on the Earth. The seven continents are: North America, Europe, Asia, South America, Africa, Australia, and Antarctica.

distortion A change in shape from how something really looks.

equator The starting point for measuring latitude. The equator is at 0° latitude and separates the Earth into Northern and Southern hemispheres.

globe A sphere with a map of the Earth on it.

hemisphere Half of the Earth. The Earth is divided into four hemispheres—Northern, Southern, Eastern, and Western.

latitude The distance north or south of the equator measured in degrees.

longitude The distance east or west of the prime meridian measured in degrees.

prime meridian The starting point for measuring longitude. The prime meridian is at 0° longitude and separates the Earth into Eastern and Western hemispheres.

Index